FRIENDS FOREVER

Thank you for choosing us! This book is the fourteenth creation of NPN Press. I'm a mother of three determined to provide meaningful products that, at the same time, can be educational and have great quality.

My granny used to say that with the right amount of time, effort and love, any dish would turn out delicious. Let's hope this formula can also be applied into the book you are now holding in your hands.

If you have any suggestions on how to keep improving our products or you want to stay up to date with our new releases, please check the QR code at the end of the book or write us at npnpress@mareninja.com

Since we are a small family business your support means the world to us. **Please, leave a comment on the Amazon page of this book or recommend it to your loved ones!**

IN LOVING MEMORY OF:

Hi!

My name is Natalie. If you are reading this is because you lost someone special in your life, I'm sorry. But you are lucky to have another someone special who cares for you so much that has gifted you this book

You know what? I've also lost dear people and animals, friends and family. And it is sad, painful, sometimes maddening even, but it can also be beautiful.

With this book I want to try to help you organise some of your best memories with your lost friend, so you can remember your friendship forever. From time to time, you will also find pages that are dedicated just for you and your feelings. Us humans often are very complicated creatures and big or small, young or old, we all need help dealing with our emotions.

You can fill the pages in this book in any order you want. You can chose to fill some and leave some empty. This is a space of love. There is no right or wrong. No judgement. No expectations. Just love, for you and your friend.

Natalie
xxxx

"There is no footprint too small to leave an imprint on this world. "

You can draw or stick a picture of both of you

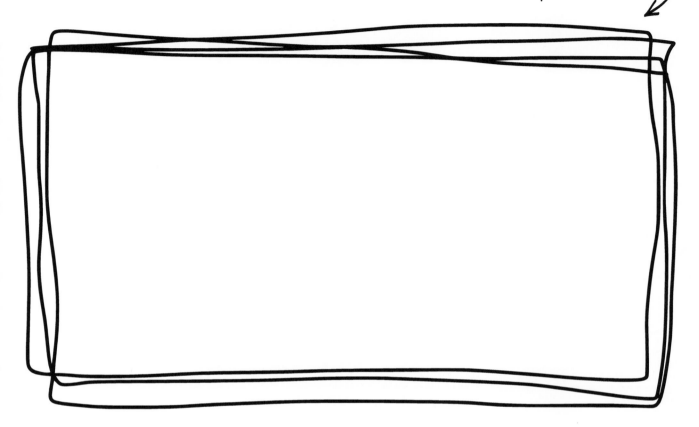

First of all, introductions!

Your name:

Your pet's name:

Do you remember who picked the name?

Tell the story behind the name!
Why this name and not another?

BIRTHDAY TIME!

Your birthday date:

Your pet's birthday date:

Who was older?

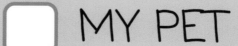 MY PET

 ME

ANIMAL GROUP

To which animal group did your pet belong?

Circle the option that applies

Mammals

Birds

Fish

Reptiles

Amphibians

Invertebrates

What are the basic traits of that group?

GRIEF

What am I feeling?

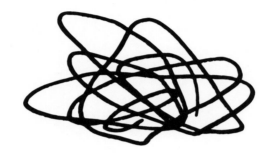

Grief is a feeling that we experience when we lose someone or something that is important to us. You just lost a very special friend and that is very painful.

Grief can make us feel sad, angry, confused, and even scared. We might cry, feel sick, or have trouble sleeping or eating. Sometimes, we might feel like we don't want to do anything or be around anyone. All of these feelings and reactions are normal and okay.

Grief is a process that takes time, and everyone experiences it differently. It's important to understand that there's no right or wrong way to grieve, and that it's okay to feel whatever we're feeling.

It's also important to talk about our feelings and memories with someone we trust. This can be a family member, friend, or even a counselor or therapist. They can listen to us and help us work through our emotions.

Remember, grief can be hard, but it's a natural and normal part of life. Luckily, grief won't last forever, it will just stay with us for a while. So don't worry if, right now, you only feel sad emotions, it's completely normal. Please be kind to yourself and ask for help when you need it.

HIS FIRST DAY

What do you remember about
your first day together?

IN LATIN

In the scientific world, all animals have a latin name. For example, wolves are called Canis Lupus or honey bees are Apis Mellifera. What is the latin name of the species of your pet?

MOVIE STAR

Imagine your friend would be the star of a new movie...

Movie title:

Genre:

Movie plot:

EMOTION EXPRESSION :

SADNESS

Feel free to scribble, draw, write, paint, collage...

Sadness is a feeling that we all experience from time to time. It's a normal and natural emotion that happens when something doesn't go as we hoped or expected, or when we lose something or someone that we care about

.

When we're sad, it's okay to cry, to talk to someone about how we're feeling, or to take some time to ourselves to feel better. It's important to know that feeling sad doesn't mean that we're weak or that there's something wrong with us.

It's also important to know that sadness is a feeling that comes and goes, just like all of our other emotions. It's okay to feel sad sometimes, the same way it's okay to feel happy and excited other times.

And it's also completely fine to mix emotions. Laughing while being sad doesn't mean you are less sad than someone crying all the time.

**Most important:
Be kind to yourself when being sad**

FEELING GOOD

Sometimes when we experience grief, it can feel like we are only surrounded by sad emotions and thoughts. That's why it's very important to find things that can bring us a little bit of joy so we can feel more balanced. And please, never ever feel guilty to feel joy while grieving. Emotions don't compete against each other, they work together.

Some activities that might help you feel better are:

- Listen to upbeat music
- Eat comforting food
- Get out into nature
- Spend quiet time in your room
- Watch a funny movie or series
- Get a hug from a loved one
- Dance or do some sport
- Play with friends

A LITTLE POEM

When your special friend has passed away,
And you feel sad day after day,
Remember the love that you both shared,
The happy moments that you once paired.

Though they may not be with you now,
Their memory will always somehow,
Live on in your heart and your mind,
A special place where they'll always find.

So don't be afraid to shed a tear,
Grieve as long as you need to, my dear,
But know that your pet is at rest,
In a place where they feel their best.

And when you think of them each day,
Remember the joy that they brought your way,
For your pet will always be with you,
In memories that are kind and true.

♥

Free to use it as you like.

TREATS

What kind of treats were your pet's favourite?

Why don't you get a treat for
yourself after finishing this page?
You deserve it!

ADJECTIVES

List some adjectives that come to mind when you think about your pet. They can describe external traits or character. When you're finished, tick the ones you share!

- [ ] _____
- [ ] _____
- [ ] _____
- [ ] _____
- [ ] _____
- [ ] _____
- [ ] _____
- [ ] _____
- [ ] _____
- [ ] _____

Did you look much alike?

Did you have the same personality?

What trait did your pet have that you wish you would have too?

Sometimes, we realise that we don't need to share many similarities with anyone in order for us to love or be loved. Everyone is unique and we should cherish it.

Now, let's list some of your favourite adjectives
about yourself!

 I am...

SLEEPING TIME

z z z

Did you sleep together?

☐ YES ☐ NO

How many hours do you usually sleep per day?

....

How many hours did your pet usually sleep per day?

....

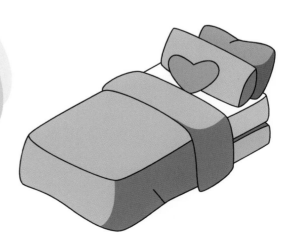

EMOTION EXPRESSION :
ANGER

Feel free to scribble, draw, write, paint, collage...

Anger is a feeling that we all have sometimes. It's a normal and natural emotion that happens when we feel upset or frustrated about something, like the death of a loved one.

When we're angry, it's okay to feel our emotions and express how we feel, but it's important to do so in a safe and respectful way. It's also important to know that feeling angry doesn't mean that we're bad or that there's something wrong with us. It's a normal part of being human.

However, we must learn how to manage our anger so that we don't hurt ourselves or others. We can do this by taking a break when we feel ourselves getting angry, counting to ten, taking deep breaths, or going for a walk to cool down.

If we're having a hard time managing our anger, it can be helpful to talk to someone we trust.

**Most important:
Be kind to yourself when being mad**

Free to use it as you like.

 # BEING FUNNY

Tell a funny story about your pet.

HA HA

TRAVEL TIME

Did you travel together?

Write down some of your favourite places, but if you didn't get that chance, write down where would you have loved to travel together.

Stick or draw some
pictures of your travels.

Write about some real travel memories or
use your imagination to plan a fun one!

SUPER HERO TIME

What would its Superhero name be?

And yours?

Superpowers list

----------------   ----------------

----------------   ----------------

----------------   ----------------

WORDS LEFT UNSPOKEN

Sometimes, when loved ones disappear from our lives we realise there are things (words and feelings) that we still need to tell them. Some things we might have never told them before and others maybe not enough times. It doesn't matter if it's profound or silly, poetic or simple... This is a safe space for your words and feelings.

EMOTION EXPRESSION :
FEAR

Feel free to scribble, draw, write, paint, collage...

Fear is a feeling that we all experience sometimes. It's a normal and natural emotion that happens when we feel like we're in danger, when we're faced with something that we don't understand or when we are worried about something.

When we're feeling afraid, it's okay to tell someone we trust, like a parent or teacher. They can help us feel safe and help us understand what's going on. It's also okay to take a break or step back from the situation that is causing our fear, so we can calm down and feel more comfortable.

It's important to know that feeling afraid is a normal part of being human, that there's nothing to be ashamed of and it doesn't mean that we're weak or that there's something wrong with us. Everyone gets scared sometimes, and it's okay to talk about our fears and ask for help if we need it.

**Most important:
Learn how to manage fear so that it doesn't prevent us from doing things that are important to us**

EATING TIME

Would you eat your pet's food?

☐ YES   ☐ NO

How many times do you usually have a meal per day?

....

How many times did your pet usually eat per day?

....

YOUR FAVOURITE FOODS

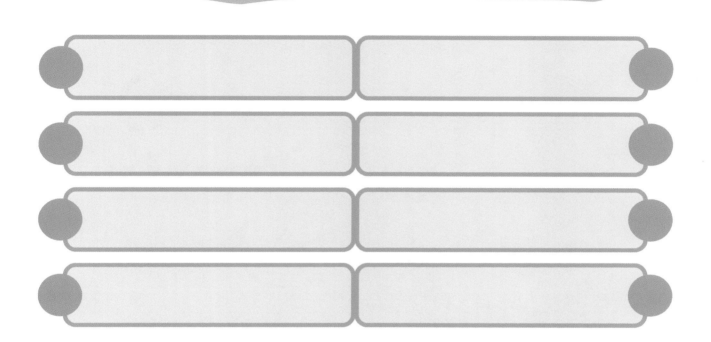

FOODS YOU WOULD LIKE TO AVOID AT ALL COSTS

SING IT, BABY!

Imagine your friend would be the lead singer of a new music band...

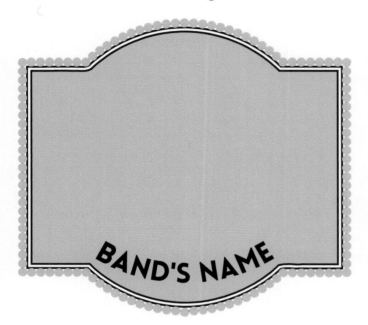

BAND'S NAME

Type of music

GREATEST HITS

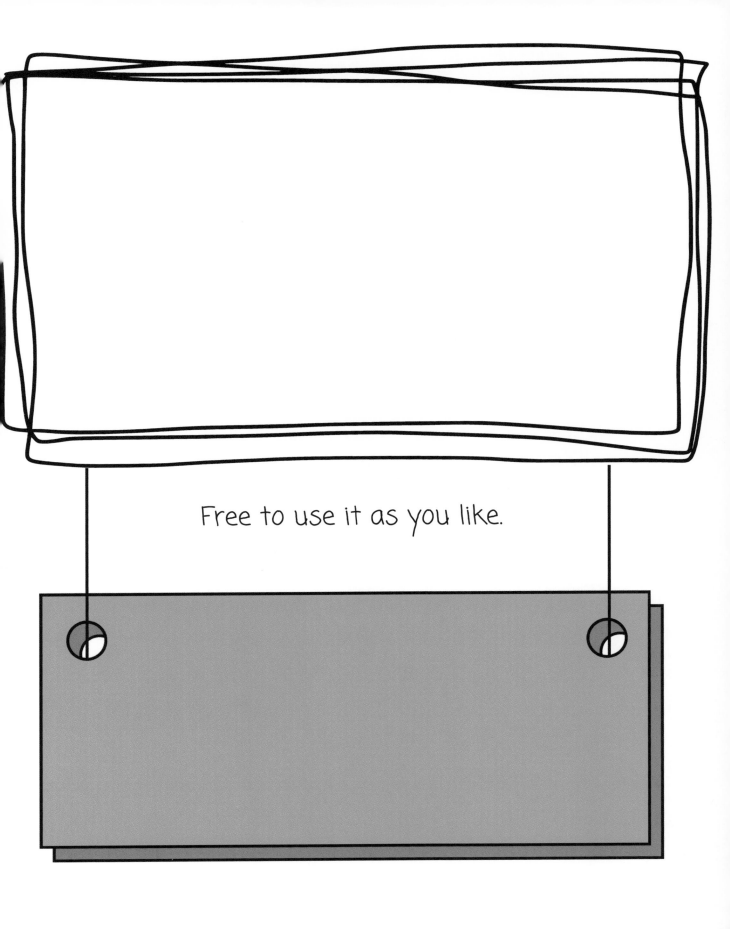

Free to use it as you like.

SPECIAL PLACE

Was there a place you liked to go when you were together? Did you have a secret hideout place? Is there any place where you feel more connected to your friend?

If possible, try to visit this place when you feel you need extra comfort with your sadness or when you need to feel closer to your lost friend.

But if you physically can't go to this place or sadly this place doesn't exist for you, don't worry. Close your eyes and imagine a place where you would have a great time playing there with your friend.

Got it? Perfect! Now you have a happy place available to you anytime! Just close your eyes and off you go!

BEING NAUGHTY OOPS!

Do you remember a time when your pet was a little bit naughty?

EMOTION EXPRESSION :

JOY

Feel free to scribble, draw, write, paint, collage...

Joy is a feeling that we all experience sometimes. It's a happy and excited feeling that happens when something good happens or when we're doing something that we really enjoy.

When we're feeling joy, it's okay to express our happiness and share our joy with others. For example, we might laugh, smile, or do a happy dance.

However, it's also important to remember that joy isn't the only emotion we'll feel and that it would not be healthy to try to just feel joy and block all other emotions.

If we're feeling joyful, it's important to enjoy the moment and share our happiness with others. And if we're feeling down, we can remember the times when we felt joyful and do things that help us feel happy again, like spending time with loved ones or doing something creative.

**Most important:
Enjoy and share joy while it lasts**

HIS LAST DAY

Feel free to express anything that comes to mind about that day

----

LIFE CELEBRATION

Many people don't know the exact birthday date of their pets but they all remember the date of their passing. Why don't we use this opportunity to celebrate their life and remember them forever?

Mark in your calendar the date when your friend died and each year take the time to honour their memory. It will be a good time to recall your best anecdotes together, look at some pictures...

Maybe reading this book once a year can help you remember the best things about your friendship but also show you if your feelings and emotions have evolved or remain the same.

WISHES FROM NOW ON

Write some of your hopes and wishes for the afterlife of your beloved friend.

"HOW LUCKY I AM TO HAVE SOMETHING THAT MAKES SAYING GOODBYE SO HARD"

WINNIE THE POOH

EXTRA SPACE

Feel free to use the next pages
however you want. You can stick
photos, write more memories, a
poem...

Printed in Great Britain
by Amazon

39205479R00032